Crossing a Continent

5 PTAS

IV CENTENARIO DE

FLORIDA

CABEZA
DE VACA

CORREOS

ESPAÑA

Courtesy of the Florida State Archives

Crossing a Continent

The Incredible Journey of
Cabeza de Vaca

Lissa Johnston

EAKIN PRESS ⊽ɛ⫿ Austin, Texas

FIRST EDITION
Copyright © 2005
By Lissa Johnston
Published in the United States of America
By Eakin Press
A Division of Sunbelt Media, Inc.
P.O. Drawer 90159
Austin, Texas 78709-0159
email: sales@eakinpress.com
⌨ website: www.eakinpress.com ⌨
ALL RIGHTS RESERVED.
1   2   3   4   5   6   7   8   9
1-57168-183-3

Library of Congress Cataloging-in-Publication Data

Johnston, Lissa Jones.
  Crossing a continent : the incredible journey of Cabeza de Vaca /
Lissa Jones Johnston.
    p. cm.
  Includes bibliographical references.
  Summary: An account of the trouble-plagued expedition that led
Spanish explorer Cabeza de Vaca from Santo Domingo to Florida to Texas
to Mexico at the end of the sixteenth century.
  ISBN 1-57168-183-3
  1. Núñez Cabeza de Vaca, Alvar, 16th cent.–Juvenile literature. 2.
Explorers–America–Biography–Juvenile literature. 3. Explorers–Spain–
Biography–Juvenile literature. 4. America–Discovery and exploration–
Spanish–Juvenile literature. [1. Cabeza de Vaca, Alvar Núñez, 16th cent.
2. Explorers. 3. America–Discovery and exploration–Spanish.] I. Núñez
Cabeza de Vaca, Alvar, 16th cent.   II. Title.
E125.N9J65   1997
970.01'6–dc21   97-32648
                                                                                        CIP
                                                                                        AC

Contents

Foreword

What would you do?

Imagine yourself preparing for the adventure of a lifetime. You have always dreamed of traveling to a mysterious land. Finally, you are about to get your chance. You have never been to this place before; few people have. But you have heard the stories of those who have ventured there and back, and you cannot wait to go. These stories include tales of fame and fortune. It could be dangerous, but you are willing to risk it.

The day finally arrives when you set forth on your journey. You have everything you think you will need: money, food, clothing, and some weapons, just in case. Many others are traveling with you, and everyone is excited to be off. But it is a long journey. Things start to go wrong long before you reach your destination. Some of your fellow travelers are ready to return home, but you are determined to continue.

After many months of hard travel, you arrive. Nothing is as you imagined. Instead of a paradise filled with riches, you find a harsh land filled with hostile natives. One disaster after another befalls your group, until finally only you and a handful of others remain. You are virtually alone in a land you know very little about, left only with the rags on your back. You have no map, no food or water, no money, and you do not understand a word the natives say.

What would you do? How would you get home?

This is the situation in which Alvar Nuñez Cabeza de Vaca found himself, shipwrecked on the shore of Texas in November of 1528. He wandered across the American Southwest for eight years before he found a Spanish outpost. He and his three companions were the first Europeans to cross the North American continent. His is a tale of adventure, hardship, and perseverance.

Fortunately for us, he wrote down everything that happened to him for the king of Spain to read. This book is based on those writings.

Chapter 1

Born to Explore

Alvar Nuñez Cabeza de Vaca was born around 1490 in the Spanish town of Jerez de la Frontera, near the larger city of Cádiz. His last name, "Cabeza de Vaca," means "cow's head." This may seem like a strange name, but his family was very proud of it.

Long before he was born, one of Cabeza de Vaca's relatives used the skull of a cow as a marker to show his king a secret mountain pass. The secret pass helped the king and his army to win a battle with the Moors, enemies of Spain from Africa. Cabeza de Vaca's ancestors were proud of their role in defeating the Moors. They showed their pride by adding a picture of a cow's skull to their family crest.

You could say that Cabeza de Vaca was born to explore. His grandfather, Pedro de Vera Mendoza, was the conqueror of the Grand Canary Islands. Cabeza de Vaca was raised in his grandfather's home. It is easy to imagine the boy listening to his grandfather's tales of the conquest, dreaming of following in his footsteps. There were many slaves from the Canary Islands in the household. Cabeza de Vaca felt comfortable around these exotic people, so different in looks and language.

Cabeza de Vaca was lucky to be born at about the some time that the Age of Discovery began. Much of the credit for this new era of exploration can go to Prince Henry of Portugal, later known as Prince Henry the Navigator. With a keen interest in exploration, he hired the best mapmakers, sailors, and shipbuilders. Their headquarters was not far from where Cabeza de Vaca grew up.

These experts came up with new designs for ships to sail longer, farther, and faster. By using these new ships, explorers made many exciting discoveries:

- Columbus landed in the New World in 1492.
- Vasco da Gama sailed around Africa to discover a sea route to India in 1498.
- Hernan Cortes conquered the Aztec empire of Mexico in 1521.
- Ferdinand Magellan's attempt to sail around the world was completed by one of his ships in 1522.

New World discoveries brought Spain great wealth in gold, silver, and spices. These riches helped make Spain the most powerful nation in Europe and provided the means for bigger expeditions. People were very excited about joining the expeditions. Everyone wanted to be the next Columbus or Cortes. Cabeza de Vaca was no exception.

When he was a young man, Cabeza de Vaca served as a soldier for the king of Spain. He traveled as far as Italy, and fought in one of the bloodiest battles of that time. When he returned to Spain, he married and went to work for a duke in the city of Seville.

This was the perfect city for a young man who dreamed of exploration. It was the main site of trading between Spain and the New World. Many expeditions began and ended here by sailing down the Guadalquivir River to the Atlantic Ocean. Ferdinand Magellan spent two years in Seville, preparing for his famous voyage around the world. Christopher Columbus also lived in Seville for a short time.

The latest arrival of an expedition from the New World was very exciting for the people of Seville.

Everyone wanted to be the next Columbus or Cortes. Cabeza de Vaca was no exception.

They would rush to the wharf to see what amazing new cargo would be unloaded. They might see animals strange and new to them, such as parrots, monkeys, and llamas. Most fascinating of all was the arrival of natives from the New World. The people of Seville were the first in Europe to get a glimpse of them. They were so different, with their brown skin, long black hair, and exotic clothing.

Cabeza de Vaca dreamed of the day when he could see these natives in their own land.

Chapter 2
Starting Out

The day finally came in February of 1527. King Charles V of Spain appointed Cabeza de Vaca treasurer of an expedition led by a man named Panfilo de Narváez. Being treasurer was very important. He would be responsible for the king's profits from the trip. King Charles chose Cabeza de Vaca for this job because he was honest, he was good at math, and the king knew he could trust him. Cabeza de Vaca was also provost marshal for the journey, in charge of making sure the soldiers obeyed orders.

King Charles wanted Narváez to explore and settle the newly discovered land of Florida. He was also to explore the Gulf Coast from Florida all the way to Mexico. Many stories had been circulating about Florida, including one about a "fountain of youth."

Narváez was eager to gain glory—and fortune—by conquering this mysterious land. As leader, he was expected to provide everything: ships, equipment, food, horses, and men. King Charles merely granted permission and shared in the profits.

Their fleet of five ships set sail on June 17, 1527, from San Lúcar de Barrameda, at the mouth of the Guadalquivir River. The ships were of a type known as a *caravella redonda*. They had a combination of square and triangular sails in order to sail in a variety of winds. They were also designed to sail in the deep waters and high waves of the ocean. Larger than earlier designs, they could hold lots of supplies for the journey over, and lots of treasure on the trip back.

> **Crossing the Atlantic took weeks. There was little room to sleep or eat.**

The ships were overflowing with about 600 colonists and soldiers, plus horses, arms, and supplies. The colonists included both men and their wives.

Ocean travel was hard in the 1500s. Crossing the Atlantic usually took several weeks. There was little room to eat or sleep, or even to sit comfortably. Every square inch was needed for storing the cargo.

The sleeping areas below decks were crowded, damp, and smelly. Trunks, crates, and extra equipment pressed in from all sides. Very little fresh air came in through the entryways above. The odors of mildew, live animals, and spoiled food mixed with the body odor of crew and passengers who rarely took baths.

There was no such thing as a private bathroom. Using the bathroom was easy for the crew, as they just went over the side of the ship. If you needed to sit down, there were wooden seats attached to the front of the ship. Each seat had a hole in it and hung out over the water.

The food was bad, likely to spoil or run out—or both. Sometimes animals, such as chickens, pigs, and goats, were taken along to be killed for fresh meat. The flour for biscuits could not last long stored in the damp. It often became a home for maggots, cockroaches, and rats. The fresh water supply usually ran low or turned rancid during the journey.

Cabeza de Vaca was used to harsh conditions from the time he served in the king's army. But many of his fellow travelers had had enough. More than 140 people left the expedition at their first stop in the New World, Santo Domingo. They preferred to seek their fortune on this beautiful island paradise. The sandy beaches and fresh food appealed to them much more than getting back on board a stinking, crowded ship.

Chapter 3

The Storm

Narváez was disappointed, but he was determined to go on. He bought more supplies and horses while he had the chance. About 450 people continued to their next stop: Cuba.

Sailing from Santo Domingo, the expedition reached the port of Santiago, Cuba, in the fall of 1527. Again, they bought more supplies, arms, and horses.

Narváez received an offer of free supplies from a man living in Trinidad, on the other side of the island. Narváez sent Cabeza de Vaca with two ships and their crews to pick up the supplies before they continued to Florida. After he arrived at Trinidad, Cabeza de Vaca went into town to get the free supplies. He wanted the crews of both ships to come with him. A few agreed, but most wanted to remain on board until he returned.

While they were ashore, a hurricane struck. The rain pelted them like icy bullets. Towering waves crashed onto the shore. Howling winds knocked down entire buildings. Cabeza de Vaca and his men had to choose between staying indoors and being crushed by a falling building, or moving outside and risk being killed by a falling tree. They chose the outdoors.

Outside in the fury of the hurricane, they clung together in large groups to avoid being blown away. Trees crashed down around them. They were drenched and miserable. Cabeza de Vaca and his men wandered through the storm all night, trying to stay alive.

The next day, the storm subsided. Cabeza de Vaca and his men struggled back to Trinidad. A fearsome sight met them there. Cabeza de Vaca reported that the entire area was wiped out. The buildings were rubble, and trees were flattened. Even the grass was gone.

Fearing the worst, Cabeza de Vaca rushed to the harbor. His two ships were nowhere to be found. A small boat from one of the ships was lodged in a treetop. He discovered the bodies of two of his men washed ashore after the storm; the rest were never found. Sixty men and twenty horses were lost. The thirty or so men who came ashore with him were the only ones who survived.

The storm left Cabeza de Vaca and his men stranded. They were very low on food and supplies until Narváez finally arrived on November 5. His four ships had made it to a safe harbor before the hurricane struck. The men were still in shock from their ordeal, and everyone agreed they should spend the winter in Cuba.

Cabeza de Vaca rushed to the harbor. His two ships were nowhere to be found.

Since they wouldn't be sailing any time soon, Narváez decided to visit his wife on the other end of the island. He put Cabeza de Vaca in charge of the remaining ships and their crews. Cabeza de Vaca moved the ships to the safer port of Xagua, a few miles down the coast from Trinidad. He and his men stayed there over the winter.

At the beginning of 1528, Narváez returned to Xagua with an extra ship purchased in Trinidad. He had also hired a pilot, Diego Miruelo, who claimed to be familiar with their destination. Equipped with a new pilot, the expedition continued. Four hundred people and eighty horses sailed from Xagua on February 22, 1528.

It was not long before the crew began to wonder about the abilities of pilot Miruelo. Soon after they set sail, he ran them aground on some shallows along the Cuban coast. They were stuck there for two weeks. Finally, a strong south wind caused waves high enough to set them free. Then they sailed northwest, hitting two more bad storms. Gigantic waves crashed over them. Powerful winds threatened to tear the ships apart. The crew wrestled with the sails and rigging, trying to keep each ship afloat. They succeeded.

The storms had delayed their journey even more. When strong winds blew them toward Florida, they took advantage of them and skipped a planned stop for supplies in Havana.

Courtesy of the Florida State Archives

Chapter 4

Florida

The Florida coast came into view in April of 1528. They were somewhere near what is now Tampa Bay. Native dwellings dotted the shoreline. No doubt the crew was thrilled to start exploring Florida for fame and fortune. Little did they realize that this was the beginning of the end of the Narváez expedition.

On April 16, 1528, Panfilo de Narváez went ashore and performed a very official ceremony. He proclaimed Florida to be under the rule of King Charles V of Spain. No natives were present, but he performed the ceremony anyway. Even if they had been present, they could not have understood a word he said.

Next, the cargo and animals had to be unloaded

from the ships. The crew hauled many heavy containers of all shapes and sizes through the surf and onto the shore. Only forty-two of the eighty horses remained. But the surviving animals were too weak from their long journey to be of any use. They needed to rest and eat on dry land in order to regain their strength.

The next day some of the natives from the village came to visit the Spaniards. Cabeza de Vaca described them in his journal:

The Indians . . . in Florida are all archers. They go naked, are large of body, and appear at a distance like giants. They are of admirable proportions, very spare and of great activity and strength. The bows they use are as thick as the arm, of eleven or twelve palms in length, which they will discharge at two hundred paces with so great precision that they miss nothing.

This was quite different from seeing a few natives in the streets of Seville.

The natives gestured for the Spaniards to leave at once. Narváez ignored them, of course. The expedition had not spent close to a year traveling to Florida, only to turn around and go home.

He organized a party of forty men, including

Cabeza de Vaca, to begin exploring the area. Soon they met some more natives nearby. Using gestures, they got right to the point: Where could they find food? Was there any gold in the area? The natives finally understood what the Spaniards wanted. Also using gestures, they directed the Spaniards north to "Apalachen," where they said there was plenty of both.

Florida was very different from Spain. Cabeza de Vaca wrote that the land was very flat and had many different types of trees. The forests were filled with various types of animals. Cabeza de Vaca saw deer, rabbits, bears, and panthers. He also described one that had never been seen before.

> **The natives gestured for the Spaniards to leave at once. Narváez ignored them.**

Among [the animals of this area] we saw an animal with a pocket on its belly, in which it carries its young until they know how to seek food, and if it happened that they should be out feeding and any one come near, the mother will not run until she has gathered them in together.

This creature would later be known as the opossum.

Meanwhile, Narváez had sent the pilot, Miruelo, back to one of the ships. He was to look for a large bay. This bay was a landmark for the expedition. If they could find it, they would know they had landed in the right place. If Miruelo could not find this bay, he was to sail to Havana and return with a supply ship that had been left there.

By the first of May, Miruelo had not returned, and food was running low. The men were becoming anxious.

Narváez called a meeting with a small group of the men to discuss what should be done. He proposed to march north until they reached the large bay Miruelo spoke of. The ships were to sail along the coast with them. This bay was supposed to be very near their destination, a city called Pánuco on the Rio de las Palmas (River of Palms) in Mexico.

Narváez asked for the opinions of the others. Cabeza de Vaca thought this was a bad idea. He was against leaving the ships.

I said that it seemed to me that by no means should we leave the vessels until they were in a secure and inhabited harbor, and that he should note that the pilots were not certain, nor did they agree in any one thing, nor know where we were . . .

He also pointed out that the horses were still too weak to carry men or supplies. No one knew how to speak with the natives to learn about the area. They had no map, nor any idea where they were. And they were running low on supplies. Cabeza de Vaca thought they should all return to the ships and try to find a better place for exploration and settlement.

The others in the group supported their leader, Narváez. They had had many bad experiences at sea, and were not willing to return to the ships. Only one of the group supported Cabeza de Vaca's idea, so Narváez had his way. It would not be long before they all lived to regret this decision.

They had no idea they were hundreds of miles from Mexico.

Chapter 5

Native Encounters

Narváez wanted Cabeza de Vaca to take charge of the ships. Cabeza de Vaca refused, knowing this was only meant to punish him for disagreeing. Cabeza de Vaca was too proud to allow Narváez to get away with such a plan. He insisted on staying with the men on land.

Some of the men and all of the wives of the colonists returned to the ships. The rest of the 300 men set out marching north toward Apalachen on May 1, 1528. Each man received two pounds of biscuit and one-half pound of bacon for the journey. The food lasted only fifteen days, and they soon became weak from hunger. Whenever they reached a village, they usually found some maize to eat. Sometimes it was all they had to eat for days at a time.

The route to Apalachen was not easy. Many lakes slowed them down, and the forest floor was littered with tree trunks, charred by lightning strikes. The Spaniards struggled through swamps, forests, sand, and mud. Their shoulders were rubbed raw from carrying their heavy armor.

Natives attacked often. They threw stones and clubs, and shot arrows. They were very clever about planning their attacks. Often they waited until the Spaniards were crossing a lake. Then they would attack from out of range or when the Spaniards were unable to defend themselves. The Spaniards had trouble fighting back because the natives were so quick and well hidden.

The natives were also very strong. Their bows and arrows were powerful; their aim was excellent. Cabeza de Vaca said they hardly ever missed their target. The Spaniards' armor was of little use. A native's arrow could pierce the armor, go through the body, and come out through the armor on the other side.

The best weapon the Spaniards had was their horses. There were no horses in the New World at that time. The horses certainly made traveling

through the strange land much easier. The natives were afraid of the huge beasts.

Cabeza de Vaca and the others met many different tribes as they traveled. Once they met a chief riding on the back of one of his subjects. The chief wore a fancy painted deerskin. A group of other natives followed him, playing reed flutes.

During the march, many of the men had fallen ill due to hunger, disease, and attacks by the natives. Every man, including Cabeza de Vaca, had been injured at least once. The disease was probably malaria, carried by the mosquitoes.

When they finally reached Apalachen, they were very disappointed. The village had some food available, but there was no gold. The natives, wanting them to leave, attacked them several times. They even set fire to their own village to drive them out.

The Spaniards learned from some of these natives that Apalachen was the largest village in the area. There was another village farther along the coast called Aute. The natives said there was more food and even gold there. After staying more than three weeks to rest and eat, the Spaniards set out for Aute.

Chapter 6

Boat Builders

More than a week of hard travel through dense forest and constant threat of attack brought the Spaniards to Aute. There was indeed more food than before. The natives raised maize, beans, and pumpkins. They also had some fish to eat. But there was no gold. The Spaniards finally realized they had little chance of discovering fame or fortune in this primitive land.

Narváez called a second meeting. The men discussed various plans. After their back-breaking march through the Florida wilderness, they had had enough of travel by land. Cabeza de Vaca's earlier idea of returning to the ships was starting to sound like a good one. They decided to build some boats and return to the sea. They hoped to find their own ships, or the city of Pánuco.

At first, this plan seemed impossible. They had no supplies for building a ship. No one among them knew anything about shipbuilding or navigation. But they were desperate.

One by one, they came up with some ideas. One man suggested turning their metal items into tools. They had stirrups, spurs, and crossbows to use for this purpose. Another had an idea about making a bellows. A bellows would help them make very hot fires for melting their metal. Then they could re-shape it into tools needed to build the ships. Someone else organized trips into Aute for maize to eat. They were also forced to kill the horses for food. Cabeza de Vaca wrote that he could never eat the horse meat.

Their plan slowly began to work.

We commenced to build on the fourth [of September, 1528], with the only carpenter in the company, and we proceeded with so great diligence that on the twentieth day of September five boats were finished.

The Spaniards used everything they could think of to make the boats. They found some pine trees with sticky sap to help make the boats waterproof. The tails and manes of their horses were braided into ropes. Skin from the horses' legs was used to make water bottles. Everyone donated their shirts to be made into sails.

At last, five boats were finished. Each was about sixty-five feet long.

On September 22 they left what they called the Bay of Horses and sailed for open water. This was south of what is now Tallahassee, Florida. The 250 remaining men squeezed into the five crude boats. They were constantly on the verge of capsizing.

> Soon they ran out of fresh water. Food was also running out.

The plan was still to reach Pánuco. Hugging the coastline, they continued to search for the large bay that was to be their landmark. None of the bays they found was large enough or deep enough to be the right one. Occasionally, they spotted natives on shore or in canoes. The natives appeared hostile.

Soon they ran out of fresh water. Some men foolishly drank water from the sea. (The salt in sea water is bad for you. If you drink enough of it, it can kill you.) Food was also running out. After some time they came to where the great Mississippi River empties into the Gulf of Mexico. Cabeza de Vaca described the Mississippi River in his journals—

fourteen years before Hernando de Soto "dis-covered" it.

The thirsty Spaniards were thankful to be able to drink from the fresh water flowing into the gulf. They tried to row ashore to build a fire. They wanted to use the fresh water to boil some of their maize to eat. But the river's current was so strong, they were unable to do so. In fact, the current forced the boats farther out into the Gulf of Mexico and scattered them around.

The five boats became separated for a while. Cabeza de Vaca spotted Narváez's boat and shouted for instructions. He felt they should all try to stay together. Narváez disagreed, saying each boat should try to come ashore as best they could. He then turned away and rowed his boat toward shore. Cabeza de Vaca now understood that it was "every man for himself." He rowed toward another boat that was closer to his, and the two boats tried to stay together through the night.

After four days together, the two boats became separated during a storm. The men could hardly go on. Their daily ration of a half handful of maize was not enough for a bird, much less a man. Their clothes were now in rags, offering little protection from the chill waves and winter winds.

Finally, on the morning of November 6, 1528,

Cabeza de Vaca heard what sounded like waves crashing against the shore. Only one other man on his boat had any strength left; the others appeared near death. These two did their best to steer the boat closer to land. As they neared the shore, a powerful wave tossed their flimsy craft onto the beach. The men flew out of the boat and onto the sand. This rude shock was their welcome to the land that would be named Texas.

Remember the colonists who went aboard the ships in Florida? They sailed up and down the Florida coast, looking for those who had remained on land. During this time, one of the women on board convinced all the other women that the land force would not return. She said they had been abandoned, and they might as well choose new husbands from the men who were with them on board. The other women agreed, and that is what they did.

After looking for the men on land for over a year, they gave up and returned to New Spain (Mexico).

Chapter 7

Bad Luck in Texas

After six miserable weeks at sea, Cabeza de Vaca and his men had landed on a small island off the Texas coast. First, they built a fire to warm themselves. They also roasted and ate some of the maize that had survived the trip from Florida. Someone found some fresh drinking water. The heat and food helped them all feel a little better.

Cabeza de Vaca took charge of the situation. He chose the strongest among them, a man named Oviedo, to scout the area. He told Oviedo to climb the tallest tree around and report on whatever he could see. From the treetops, Oviedo saw a path. He climbed down and followed it to a small, deserted village. On his way back to the Spaniards, he noticed that three natives were following him. Cabeza de Vaca recalled,

Courtesy of the Florida State Archives

"Half an hour after [Oviedo returned], they were supported by 100 other Indian bowmen, who if they were not large, our fears made giants of them."

The Spaniards were too weak to defend themselves. They were only able to offer the natives a few trinkets which had survived the voyage from Florida. The natives accepted their beads and bells and gave an arrow in return. This was their way of offering friendship to the Spaniards. The natives gestured that they would bring them something to eat the next morning.

The natives returned the next morning with fish and roots for the hungry Spaniards. After a few days of rest and plenty of food, the Spaniards felt much better. They decided to try to sail for Pánuco again.

Barely out to sea, the boat capsized and two men drowned. The survivors washed ashore, their clothes in tatters. Shivering and exhausted, they quickly built another fire to warm themselves.

The natives returned that evening with more food. The Spaniards looked so dreadful, the natives became frightened. They wanted to return to their village immediately. Cabeza de Vaca somehow managed to explain to them what had happened with the boat. He convinced them to stay. The natives then began howling and wailing over their new friends' bad luck.

With the natives carrying on in the background, the Spaniards discussed what to do next. Cabeza de Vaca suggested that they move in with the natives. At least in their village they would have food and shelter. His men disagreed, fearing for their lives. But Cabeza de Vaca insisted, feeling they had no choice.

They finally agreed to ask the natives to take them in. The natives agreed. The Spaniards did not realize the price they would pay for their survival.

The natives saw how miserable and cold the Spaniards were. They sent some of their own people ahead to prepare shelter for the newcomers. They also built fires along the way. Helping the Spaniards down the path, the natives stopped every so often to give the Spaniards a chance to warm themselves.

At the village they were provided a hut of their own, with a fire already lit inside. The Spaniards huddled together in fear while the natives danced and sang all night. They thought the celebration was in preparation for their sacrifice, but it was not. Imagine their relief when the natives arrived the next morning to feed them, not to kill them.

Cabeza de Vaca soon discovered that some of the other boats had also made it to the Texas shore. The survivors were living with a different group of natives on the other end of the same island. The two groups of Spaniards soon got together and tried to use the last remaining boat to sail for Pánuco again. But the boat sank right away, and they were forced to make other plans.

The Spaniards huddled together in fear while the natives danced and sang all night.

They decided to stay on the island until spring. But they sent four men south along the coast to look for help. These men were the strongest, and the best swimmers, among them. They left right away. The rest remained with the natives.

It was late fall, 1528. The weather soon turned colder, and everyone suffered—especially the

Spaniards. Five of them chose to live alone near the beach. When one of their group died, they had no choice but to eat the body or starve. Much later, when the natives found out about this, they were very angry. If they had caught the Spaniards doing this, they probably would have killed them for it.

Of the eighty or so men who had made it to shore in the two makeshift boats, only fifteen remained alive. The Spaniards realized their luck had not changed since leaving Florida. They named the island *Malhado*, meaning "bad luck."

Chapter 8

From Slave to Trader

The two groups of Spaniards remained separately with their own tribes. Cabeza de Vaca's men lived with natives he called *"Capoques."* The other group lived with those called the *"Hans."*

Soon after the Spaniards joined the native villages, the natives insisted that they attempt healing the sick. This would be in return for the food and shelter they had shared. They thought these strangers might have special powers. Actually, the Spaniards knew nothing of medicine, but this did not matter to their hosts. The Spaniards agreed to the natives' demands. They had no choice.

By watching carefully, the Spaniards figured out what was expected of them. One method of healing was to blow breath on the painful area. Cabeza de Vaca wrote:

> *Our method was to bless the sick, breathing upon them, and recite a Pater-noster and an Ave-Maria, praying with all earnestness to God our Lord that he would give health and influence them to make us some good return. . . . For this the Indians treated us kindly; they deprived themselves of food that they might give to us, and presented us with skins and some trifles.*

Their careers as healers were brief. It wasn't long before the natives decided the Spaniards were more useful as slaves. They were beaten, kicked, and threatened. The native children enjoyed yanking their beards. Since the natives did not have much hair anywhere on their bodies, except for their heads, beards were something new to them.

The natives forced the Spaniards to dig roots until their fingers bled. (Roots were the only food supply between October and February.) They hauled firewood on their naked backs, and the natives used them as pack animals when they moved every three or four days. It was against native custom for the men to carry anything. Only women, the elderly, and slaves performed hard labor.

When spring finally arrived, the Spaniards living with the Hans decided to leave the tribe and search for Pánuco. There were about a dozen men, led by Andrés Dorantes. At this time Cabeza de Vaca was ill with a fever. He was too weak to see Dorantes and his men when they came to say goodbye. Everyone thought Cabeza de Vaca would die. They left him behind with two others.

> Everyone thought Cabeza de Vaca would die. But he did not die.

But Cabeza de Vaca did not die. When he got better, he learned that most of the Spaniards had left. He felt he must stay with the Capoques until he could figure out a plan to find the other Spaniards.

Spending many months with the Capoques allowed Cabeza de Vaca to observe them closely. He described the people of Malhado in his journal.

The people we found there are large and well formed; they have no other arms than bows and arrows, in the use of which they are very dexterous. The men have one of their nipples bored from side to side, and some have both, wearing a cane in each, the length of two palms and a half, and the thickness of two fingers. They have the under lip also bored, and wear in it a piece of cane the breadth of half a finger. Their women are accustomed to great toil. . . . Those people love their offspring the most of any in the world, and treat them with the greatest mildness.

Cabeza de Vaca lived with the Capoques for more than a year. They were very cruel to him, and he wanted to escape. He came up with the idea of becoming a trader among the various tribes living in the area.

Accordingly, I put myself to contriving how I might get over to the other Indians, among whom matters turned somewhat more favorable for me. I set to trafficking, and strove to make my employment profitable in the ways I could best contrive, and by that means I got food and good treatment. The Indians would beg me to go from one quarter to another for things of which they have need; for in consequence of incessant hostilities, they cannot traverse the country, nor make many exchanges. With my merchandise and trade I went into the interior forty or fifty leagues.

Life as a trader was much better than as a slave. Other tribes were always interested in his wares: sea shells, skins, beans, ochre for coloring their faces, tools, and items used for making bows and arrows. He traveled far, always looking for signs of Spanish settlements. While he was traveling, he did not have to perform the hard work forced upon him by the Capoques.

Cabeza de Vaca's plan worked. The Capoques were happy to have their own trader. They let him trade among the many tribes of southern Texas. He had many chances to escape, but one thing kept him from leaving. There was one Spaniard remaining with the Capoques, Oviedo. Every year, Cabeza de Vaca stopped in his village and begged him to escape with him. Every year, Oviedo refused. It took almost six years for Oviedo to agree to leave.

Cabeza de Vaca's plan was to cross from Malhado to the mainland. There they met with some natives near a bay called Espiritu Santo. These natives had heard of other white men farther south. Of those who had set out from Malhado six years earlier, only three remained. Their new masters treated them cruelly.

We asked how the living were situated, and they answered that they were very ill used, the

boys and some of the Indian men being very
idle, out of cruelty gave them many kicks,
cuffs, and blows with sticks; that such was the
life they led ... and that we might know what
they told us of the ill usage to be true, they
slapped my companion and beat him with a
stick, and I was not left without my portion.
Many times they threw lumps of mud at us,
and every day they put their arrows to our
hearts, saying that they were inclined to kill us
in the way that they had destroyed our friends.

Oviedo feared for his life and returned to
Malhado. But Cabeza de Vaca was determined to
move on and find out who these survivors were. He
stayed with this new tribe, the Quevenes.

Chapter 9

News from Old Friends

Two days later, the Quevenes joined some other tribes to gather pecans. Cabeza de Vaca was delighted to find his fellow Spaniards among them. They were Captain Andres Dorantes, Captain Alonzo del Castillo, and Dorantes' Moor slave, Estevanico. All three were amazed to see the old friend they had given up for dead six years earlier. Cabeza de Vaca wrote, "We gave many thanks at seeing ourselves together, and this was a day to us of the greatest pleasure we had enjoyed in life."

The Quevenes gave Cabeza de Vaca to the same tribe who had Dorantes, the Mariames. Castillo and Estevanico lived with a neighboring tribe, the Yguases.

Now that they were together again, they brought

each other up to date. Cabeza de Vaca told of his career as a trader among the coastal tribes. Dorantes had news of the three other boats that had set sail from Florida so long ago.

One boat they found washed ashore as they made their way south from Malhado. They tried to use it to sail to Pánuco, but it capsized. Six of their group drowned before they could get back to shore.

The survivors found a group of natives eating mulberries. A Spaniard named Figueroa was among them. Figueroa was one of the four sent south soon after the two boats first landed on Malhado. These four had become so cold and hungry, they didn't get very far. Only Figueroa and a man named Mendez survived. Natives soon captured them, killing Mendez as he tried to escape.

Figueroa discovered that a Spaniard named Esquivel was with the Mariames. Esquivel told him what happened to two of the three remaining boats. One of the two capsized. The other, that of Governor Narváez, landed. Narváez returned to sea and rescued the others, then went back to his boat for the night. During the night, the boat was swept out to sea. He and the two men with him were never seen again.

Esquivel was one of the survivors of these two boats. One by one, he said, the men had died of cold, hunger, and illness. Again, the survivors ate the bodies of their dead in order to survive. Finally, only Esquivel remained. He was found by an Indian and became a slave until he escaped to the Mariames. Figueroa tried to convince Esquivel to escape with him, but Esquivel refused. Esquivel was later killed after one of the Mariame women dreamed Esquivel would kill her son.

Figueroa had escaped from one tribe after another. Along with the expedition's priest, he had headed south. No one knew where they were, or even if they were alive.

> Now only four survivors remained. They began to plan their escape.

The Narváez expedition began with 600 men. Only 300 went ashore in Florida. Now only Dorantes, Castillo, Estevanico, and Cabeza de Vaca remained. The four survivors were determined to reach their goal: to find a Spanish settlement.

They began to plan their escape. All of them knew it would be risky. Many of their fellows had died trying. Cabeza de Vaca tells us about his friends' warning: "They advised me on no account to let the natives know or have a suspicion of my desire to go on, else they would destroy me . . ."

The Spaniards knew that in six months, many different tribes would gather to pick prickly pears. This would be their best chance to escape. According to Cabeza de Vaca, "The prickly pear is the size of a hen's egg, vermillion and black in color, and of agreeable flavor. The natives live on it three months in the year, having nothing beside." He also said that the natives thought some types tasted better than others.

To Cabeza de Vaca, they all tasted good. He was too hungry to be picky.

Chapter 10

Starving and Observing

Six months passed. By the summer of 1533, Cabeza de Vaca and his friends were ready with their plan of escape. But the Mariames and the Yguases had a disagreement over a woman and left the prickly pear fields unexpectedly. The four Spaniards were separated again. They had to wait another year for the annual gathering before they could escape.

It was a hard year for Cabeza de Vaca. The natives worked him nearly to death, and he was always starving. Three times, the natives threatened to kill him and he had to run away. Each time, they caught him and brought him back. He must have been more valuable to them alive, for they spared his life.

During this year, Cabeza de Vaca again observed the natives carefully. He wanted to make a full report to the king of Spain if he survived. His remarks about the Yguases, masters of Castillo and Estevanico, tell us about what they ate when it wasn't prickly pear season.

Occasionally they kill deer, and at times take fish; but the quantity is so small and the famine so great, that they eat spiders and the eggs of ants, worms, lizards, salamanders, snakes, and vipers that kill whom they strike; and they eat earth and wood, and all that there is, the dung of deer, and other things that I omit to mention; and I honestly believe that were there stones in that land they would eat them.

The Yguases and many other tribes had adapted to this harsh land. They had learned to survive against great odds. In fact, they were a very hardy people in superb physical condition. This is hard to believe, considering what little they had to eat.

These Indians are so accustomed to running, that without rest or fatigue they follow a deer from morning to night. In this way they kill many. They pursue them until tired down, and sometimes overtake them in the race.

In addition to deer, Cabeza de Vaca noted that cattle roamed this area. He may be the first person to describe the bison. He described their small horns, their long fur, and the fine quality of their meat. The local natives used the meat and hide of the bison for food and clothing.

The warm summer weather ripened the prickly pears, providing enough fruit for everyone. But it also brought an unwelcome guest: the mosquito.

> The warm summer weather brought an unwelcome guest: the mosquito.

Cabeza de Vaca relates the local method of dealing with these pests. The coastal tribes used a smelly solution of shark oil as an insect repellent. Farther inland, the natives burned green wood in small fires surrounding their encampment. The green wood smoked as it burned, driving the biting insects away. However, the heat and smoke from these fires were almost as bad as having the mosquitoes around. During the summer, it was not uncommon to see people covered with the red, itchy bites from head to toe. "From my own experience, I can state there is no torment known in this world that can equal it," said Cabeza de Vaca.

Chapter 11

The Healers

In the summer of 1534, the tribes again gathered at the prickly pear fields. During this second season of coming to the prickly pear fields, Cabeza de Vaca at last learned the fate of the fifth boat.

According to one of the tribes at the prickly pear fields, the boat and its occupants washed ashore. They were killed at once by a hostile tribe living on the coast.

Once he arrived at the gathering, Cabeza de Vaca passed the word to the others: meet the night of September's full moon and be ready to escape. He was determined to go, with or without them.

The night of the full moon, his friends met him as planned. The Spaniards traveled away from the natives as fast as they dared, fearing the natives would find out they were gone and come after them. They soon saw smoke ahead and found themselves in the camp of the Avavares.

The Avavares were friendly and treated the newcomers well. They even had news of Figueroa and the priest traveling with him, who had passed through on their way south. This was the last the four Spaniards ever heard of their brave countrymen.

The Avavares were happy to have the Spaniards join them. They had heard of the Spaniards' healing skills. They brought a man complaining of headaches and asked the Spaniards to heal him.

None of the four was trained as a doctor. But they had all lived with the natives long enough to know what was expected of them.

Castillo knelt over the Indian and blew on the area that was causing the pain. He then made the sign of the cross. He added some words taught to him as a child growing up in the Catholic church. Castillo was as surprised as anyone when the Indian smiled, got up, and indicated the pain was gone. The Avavares were very impressed and gave the Spaniards many prickly pears and even some venison in payment.

From that point the Spaniards resumed their careers as healers among the natives. And their situation soon began to improve.

The Avavares brought many others in for healing. The Spaniards stayed busy and earned more prickly pears and venison than they could eat. They didn't know why their healing worked. They were just glad to be able to help the Avavares, who treated them so well.

Not long after joining this new tribe, Cabeza de Vaca was out looking for food and stayed gone until dark. He became lost and was gone for five days. He was lucky to find a burning tree that must have been struck by lightning. Taking a few of the burning limbs with him, he made a fire to help him keep warm during the night. The next day, he gathered as much firewood as he could find. He knew he would need wood for a fire if he wanted to stay alive. Also, his friends might see the smoke and come to his rescue.

> The Spaniards didn't know why their healing worked. They were just glad to be able to help.

Each night he made four fires and dug a shallow pit in the middle of the fires. He would lie in the pit and cover himself with straw to keep warm. One night he almost burned to death when his straw "blanket" caught a spark from one of his fires. He escaped with only some singed hair.

During the five days he was lost, he had nothing to eat. His feet were bare and bleeding. If a bad storm had hit during this time, he probably would have died.

On the fifth day, he found a river. Some of the Avavares were nearby. Everyone was glad to see him. They thought he might have been killed by a rattlesnake bite.

Once prickly pear season was over, the Avavares returned to their homes. The Spaniards decided to spend the winter with this friendly tribe. They would continue their search for Pánuco in the spring.

Each man took his turn at healing. Cabeza de Vaca tells of the time he was asked to heal a man who appeared to be dead. He performed the usual ritual of breathing on the man and speaking the words of the Catholic religion over him. Everyone was amazed to see the Indian up and walking around later that evening! The Avavares treated the Spaniards very well throughout the winter because of their healing skills.

Chapter 12

Adaptation

Spring arrived. The four Spaniards decided the time was right to move on. They left the Avavares and joined a tribe called the Maliacones, and then the Arbadaos. Neither of these tribes had much to eat.

The Spaniards began to weaken and feared they would not be able to complete their journey. Desperate for food, they traded some of their meager belongings for two dogs. They did not want the dogs for pets. They needed something to eat.

The Arbadaos were poor. Cabeza de Vaca and his companions did not perform much healing for them. They continued the hard work of a slave. For many years now, they went naked as the natives did. Their lighter skin was not used to the fierce sun. Cabeza de Vaca said they shed their skin like snakes about twice a year. Their chests and shoulders were covered with blisters from the sun.

The heavy loads of firewood and other things they had to carry cut into their bare arms. As they struggled through the overgrown thickets, thorns and bushes tore at their skin. Cabeza de Vaca said sometimes he was so weak from hunger and loss of blood, he was unable to carry his load back to the village.

He also recalled that during this time, he was eager to prepare animal skins for the natives. He would scrape bits of meat off the skins and eat the scraps. This would give him strength for a day or two. The Spaniards ate all of their meat raw. Their stomachs were used to raw meat. Their bodies could not digest it well if it was cooked. Besides, if they took the time to cook their meat, one of the natives most likely would snatch it off its cooking spit and eat it first.

Cabeza de Vaca became quite good at weaving mats for the natives. The Arbadaos liked for him to do this, as it gave them more time to look for food. They used the mats to make their homes and to sleep on. Cabeca de Vaca spent time making the mats, then traded them to the natives for something to eat.

Feeling a little stronger, the Spaniards left the Arbadaos and continued their journey. They slowly made their way across southwest Texas and into Mexico. They met many different tribes of natives. Although life was hard, the Spaniards had adapted to their situation. Cabeza de Vaca grew to admire the people of this harsh land.

I believe these people see and hear better, and have keener senses than any other in the world. They are great in hunger, thirst, and cold, as if they were made for endurance of these more than other men, by habit and nature.

During this time, Cabeza de Vaca learned a new

> **Cabeza de Vaca grew to admire the people of this harsh land.**

way to make "bean soup." The natives of the Southwest ate the beans of the mesquite tree. In order to make these bitter beans taste better, they prepared them in this way: First, they dug a hole in the ground. Then they put the beans in the hole and pounded them until they were mushy. Then they would add some more dirt and stir the dirt and mush together. Adding water and dirt a little at a time, they stirred and tasted until it seemed right. The villagers all sat around the hole, dipping their hands in for a taste. This took a long time, and the natives usually made it into a special celebration. The water and dirt mixture helped make their stomachs feel full.

The Spaniards became famous among all the natives of the Southwest. Sometimes the natives left their homes to travel along with them, just to watch them heal. During this time, Cabeza de Vaca performed surgery on a native who had been wounded by an arrow. The arrowhead was still in his chest and caused him great pain. Cabeza de Vaca used his knife to cut open the skin. After probing the muscle, he found the arrowhead and cut it free. He then stitched the wound closed with a needle shaped from a deer bone.

The patient felt much better the next day. His scar was very small. The impressed villagers even wanted to keep the arrowhead that came out of the wound. They threw a big party for Cabeza de Vaca and gave him and his friends even more honor and respect. When he said he wanted to continue his journey to find more Spaniards, they helped him take the right route. Many natives wanted to come with him.

Over time, the number of natives following Cabeza de Vaca and his friends grew quite large.

Chapter 13

Signs of Spaniards

Cabeza de Vaca's plan was to head west and avoid the fierce tribes of the Mexican Gulf Coast. They hoped to find signs of Spanish settlements. Finally, they reached the west coast of Mexico sometime in the spring of 1536.

They traveled through what is now Ures, near the coast of the Gulf of California. In this area, they noticed one of the local natives wearing a curious necklace. It was made of a belt buckle and a nail from a horseshoe. After almost eight years of wandering, they had found their first hint of other Spaniards in the area. Naturally, they questioned the owner of this unusual necklace. He said he got it from others like the Spaniards, but they had returned to their ships in the Gulf of California.

The group traveled farther south along the coast. Signs of other Spaniards in the area were everywhere. They noticed that the natives were afraid of these other Spaniards. The other Spaniards had been capturing natives as slaves. The natives had deserted their villages to hide in the hills, leaving their crops to rot in the fields. This saddened Cabeza de Vaca and his men. They determined to stop this shameful practice when they finally caught up to the other Spaniards.

Every day brought the travelers closer to other Spaniards. The natives scouted the area for them and reported a party of slave hunters camped nearby.

The four discussed how they should make contact. They decided to send Cabeza de Vaca and Estevanico with a small

> The small party came upon a group of four Spaniards on horseback.

group of natives to find the slave hunters. A day later, the small party came upon a group of four Spaniards on horseback. Cabeza de Vaca and his men stepped out of the brush to meet the horsemen. It was March of 1536, near the River Sinaloa in northwest Mexico.

The four horsemen could not believe their eyes. Out of nowhere, a white man and a black man appeared in the middle of the road. Even more amazing, the white man was actually speaking to them in Spanish! Cabeza de Vaca remembered:

> *The day after I overtook four of them on horseback, who were astonished at the sight of me, so strangely habited as I was, and in company with Indians. They stood staring at me a length of time, so confounded that they neither hailed me nor drew near to make an inquiry.*

Once they got over their surprise, the horsemen introduced themselves. The leader was Captain Diego de Alcaraz. He was returning from a failed search for food and slaves.

Chapter 14

End of a Long Journey

When Castillo and Dorantes appeared with 600 more natives, Alcaraz had an idea. These natives could turn his failed mission into a success if he could capture them all. Alcaraz asked Cabeza de Vaca to convince the natives to bring his Spaniards something to eat. The natives gave some of their food to the horsemen while Cabeza de Vaca and his companions argued with Alcaraz.

The natives didn't need to speak Spanish to know that the white men were disagreeing. They waited patiently until Cabeza de Vaca returned to them. He explained that he and his three friends had finally reached the end of their journey. He asked them to return to their homes, as it was now time for them to go their separate ways. He was afraid if they stayed there too long, Alcaraz would capture them. To his relief, they agreed to return to their villages.

The refugee Spaniards went with a separate group of Alcaraz's men. It was a long hike to the Spanish camp. The men became lost and were without water for several days. Seven men died of thirst. They finally reached a village near Culiacan in what is now the state of Sinaloa, in Mexico.

Later Cabeza de Vaca learned that Alcaraz's men had taken the long way to their camp on purpose. While they were gone, Alcaraz took the 600 natives as slaves. Cabeza de Vaca was very angry and disappointed.

Word of Cabeza de Vaca's group at Culiacan was sent to Melchoir Diaz, the man in charge of the Spanish camp. He came to see them right away and was amazed by their story. Diaz apologized for what Alcaraz had done to the natives. He agreed with Cabeza de Vaca that the natives should be treated better. Diaz asked Cabeza de Vaca to help him convince the natives to return to their homes. He promised they would be treated kindly if they agreed to become Christians and obey the Spaniards.

Cabeza de Vaca believed Diaz would keep his promise to treat the natives well. He helped send a message to all the natives who were hiding. The natives trusted Cabeza de Vaca. They returned to their villages and farms. They also agreed to obey the new rulers of their land.

Meanwhile, the four Spaniards made their way south to Mexico City. The viceroy of Mexico, Antonio de Mendoza, and the Marquis de Valle, Hernan Cortes, the conqueror of Mexico, came to greet them. They were treated well and given proper clothes. Cabeza de Vaca said it was a long time before he felt comfortable in clothes or was able to sleep in a real bed.

> It was a long time before he felt comfortable in clothes or was able to sleep in a real bed.

He and his companions spent the winter in Mexico. They wrote an account of their adventures and drew a map of their journey. This map has never been found. Their stories were included in a book about the New World written by a famous Spanish writer named Oviedo.

Chapter 15

A Troubled Trip Home

Cabeza de Vaca was eager to return home, but his ship could not sail because of severe storms. On April 10, 1537, the weather cleared enough for them to be able to leave. At the last minute, Cabeza de Vaca changed ships. He thought his was too leaky to make it to Spain. He was right! Of the three ships that left the port of Vera Cruz that day, only his was sturdy enough to continue the voyage.

The other two quickly returned to port, leaking badly. They could not take a chance on sinking. Besides carrying passengers, they were loaded with treasure from the New World. This left Cabeza de Vaca's ship to carry on alone, a ripe target for pirates.

The ship sailed on to Havana, Cuba, and then to

the Bahamas. While they were ashore in the Bahamas, a bad storm blew through. Cabeza de Vaca and many of his fellow travelers were certain they would not survive the night. They were thankful to see the dawn arrive and the storm subside.

Nearing the Azores, their worst fear came to pass when a French pirate ship came into view. It chased the Spanish ship all day and into the night. The two vessels played a deadly game of hide-and-seek all night long. At one point, the pirates came close enough to fire their cannons, but missed. The next morning, Cabeza de Vaca was relieved to see part of the Portuguese fleet within rescue distance. The French ship gave up the chase, speeding away as fast as sails and oars could carry it.

> *Cabeza de Vaca finally arrived at Lisbon. He had been away from home for ten years.*

No further mishaps occurred on this journey. Cabeza de Vaca finally arrived at Lisbon on August 9, 1537, after four months at sea. He had been away from home for ten years.

❡ La relacion y comentarios del gouerna
do:Aluar nuñez cabeça de vaca, de lo acaescido en las
dos jornadas que hizo a las Indias.

Con priuilegio.

❡ E sta tassada por los señores del consejo en O chenta y cinco mrs.

Courtesy of the Florida State Archives

Afterword

What happened next?

You might think Cabeza de Vaca would be ready to relax and return to the life he had led in Spain before he joined the Narváez expedition. That would make sense. But, amazingly, he asked to return to Florida immediately with an expedition of his own!

He was disappointed to learn that another man, Hernando de Soto, had received permission to explore Florida a few months earlier. De Soto wanted Cabeza de Vaca to come with him to Florida, but he refused. He wanted to lead his own expedition.

While he was waiting for another assignment, he finished his journal. He wrote down everything that happened to him on the Narváez expedition. Then he gave it to the king of Spain. This same journal has been translated into English and is now available to us in most libraries (see bibliography).

After a long wait, Cabeza de Vaca was appointed governor of the provinces of the Rio de la Plata in what is now Paraguay. He was to sail to South America and take charge of the colony. Things were going badly there. The colony was in turmoil and on the point of starvation.

Setting sail in November of 1540, he reached Brazil four months later. His destination was the capital city of Asuncion. It was 600 miles inland. There were no roads or trails. He led 400 soldiers, plus twice that many natives, on a tough march through the South American jungle. They followed the Parana River in present-day Argentina, and were the first Europeans to see Iguacu Falls. Iguacu Falls is higher and wider than Niagara Falls.

Although his overland expedition was successful, his attempts to govern the colony were not. The Spaniards already in Asuncion were used to doing as they pleased. They treated the local natives badly. When Cabeza de Vaca tried to enforce the king's laws, the Spanish colonists rebelled. They felt he favored the natives over his own countrymen. They refused to accept him as governor and threw him in jail. He was sent back to Spain in chains in 1545.

Cabeza de Vaca had to defend himself against the false charges of some of the colonists. They claimed he had done a bad job, but his friends defended him and the charges were dropped.

Cabeza de Vaca lived the rest of his life in Spain. He was appointed royal magistrate in Seville, and in 1557 his eventful life came to an end. The latter part of his life had been troubled by the outcome of the Paraguay expedition, but none of that should overshadow his accomplishments as an explorer.

As is true even today, those who are brave enough to explore new places often make exciting discoveries. Cabeza de Vaca made the first written reference to the Mississippi River, the opossum, and the bison. He also described the cultures of some of the extinct native tribes of North America. He and his three companions were the first Europeans to cross the continent of North America, from the Gulf Coast of Florida to the western shore of Mexico.

Cabeza de Vaca's story is a lesson in survival. He had learned many important skills when he was a soldier for the king of Spain. He used these skills over and over again: when the hurricane struck Trinidad; when the expedition was starving in Florida; when he washed ashore on the Texas coast.

Once stranded in Texas among the natives, he learned new skills from them in order to survive in a new land. He could have escaped their slavery at any time, but he knew that if he left them he would probably die. Cabeza de Vaca was patient. He waited for the right time to leave. He was also loyal to his friend, Oviedo. He did not want to leave him behind.

Perhaps his most important skill was knowing how to write. When he wrote a journal of his experiences, he created a record of his journey that has lasted more than 400 years. We can read his journal and marvel at these men who survived when more than 300 of their fellow explorers did not.

Cabeza de Vaca's journal is a model of survival in a hostile world, of the power of faith and hope, and the will to survive.

Bibliography

Baskett, James N. "Study of the Route of Cabeza de Vaca," *Texas State Historical Association Quarterly*, Vol. 10.

Brownlee, W. D. *The First Ships around the World*. Minneapolis: Lerner Publications Company, 1977.

Bishop, Morris. *The Odyssey of Cabeza de Vaca*. New York: The Century Company, 1933.

Davenport, Harbert, and Joseph K. Wells. "First Europeans in Texas," *Southwestern Historical Quarterly*, Vol. 22.

Grant, Neil. *The Discoverers*. New York: Arco Publishing, Inc., 1979.

Grun, Bernard. *The Timetables of History*. New York: Touchstone (Simon & Schuster), 1979.

*Hodge, Frederick W., and Theodore H. Lewis, eds. *Spanish Explorers in the Southern United States 1528-1543*. Austin, Texas: The Texas Historical Commission in Cooperation with the Center for

Studies in Texas History, The University of Texas at Austin, 1984.

McFarland, Bates H., and Brownie Ponton. "Alvar Nuñez Cabeza de Vaca," *Texas State Historical Association Quarterly,* Vol. 1.

Newcomb, W. W., Jr. *The Indians of Texas.* Austin, Texas: University of Texas Press, 1961.

Tull, Delena. *A Practical Guide to Edible and Useful Plants.* Austin, Texas: Texas Monthly Press, 1987.

*Contains a translation of the journal of Alvar Nuñez Cabeza de Vaca.

Glossary

adapted: learned how to fit in a certain environment.

Apalachen: a village of the natives of northern Florida, northeast of present-day Tallahassee.

armor: worn to protect the body against weapons; usually made of some type of metal.

arrowhead: the separate point or tip of an arrow; the type used by the natives in this story were made of stone.

Aute: a village of the natives of northern Florida near present-day Tallahassee.

bay: a part of a sea or lake pushing inward into land.

bellows: a device used to concentrate air flow.

bison: a member of the cow family with a shaggy mane, curved horns, and a humped back.

Canary Islands: a group of islands off the northwest coast of Africa.

capsize: to turn over, usually a boat.

caravel: a small, fast ship with lateen or triangular-shaped sails.

caravella redonda: a larger ship with both lateen and rectangular sails.

Columbus, Christopher: explorer famous for sailing from Europe to the New World in 1492.

Cortes, Hernan: explorer famous for the conquest of the Aztec empire in Mexico, 1519-1521.

crossbow: a weapon able to fire arrows fast and far with release of a trigger.

Cuba: largest island in the Caribbean Sea.

dexterous: skillful with one's hands.

expedition: trip or journey for some definite purpose.

extinct: no longer alive.

family crest: a design or logo representing a particular family name.

Gama, Vasco da: explorer famous for finding a sea route from Europe, around Africa, to India in 1498.

harbor: a protected area of the sea used to shelter and anchor ships.

Magellan, Ferdinand: explorer famous for his attempt to sail around the world from Spain in 1519. He was killed before he could finish, but one of his pilots did finish the trip in 1522.

maize: corn.

malaria: a disease spread by mosquitoes; causes chills and fever.

mesquite tree: a thorny tree with edible bean pods.

Moors: people of northwest Africa.

mosquito: a two-winged insect that feeds on blood.

Mexico: the country just south of the United States.

New Spain: what the Spanish called Mexico when they first came to the New World.

New World: term for Western Hemisphere, first used in the early 1500s.

ocher or ochre: a reddish-yellow clay used to color paint.

opossum: a small member of the marsupial family (this means it has a pouch) with a rat-like tail.

pack animal: any animal used to carry heavy loads for humans, such as a mule, donkey, or horse.

Panuco: near present-day Tampico, Mexico.

prickly pear: a type of cactus that is edible.

primitive: simple or basic.

provost marshal: provost means in charge; marshal means a miliatry leader. The two words together mean the chief military leader.

rancid: spoiled, ruined, rotten.

royal magistrate: magistrate means someone who has the power to make sure laws are obeyed. A royal magistrate is someone who makes sure the kings's (or queen's) laws are obeyed.

sacrifice: to give up something of value.

Santo Domingo: the capital of the Dominican Republic in the Caribbean.

shallows: shallow places in a body of water.

slave: a human who must work for and obey another person, against his or her will.

Soto, Hernando de: a Spanish explorer of the American South and Southwest, 1539-1542.

spurs: pointed, usually metal devices worn on the heel of the shoe or boot, used when riding a horse or other animal to make them go forward.

stirrups: sometimes made of metal; a ring with a flat bottom, attached to a saddle and used as a footrest.

subside: to settle down, sink, or become less agitated.

treasurer: someone in charge of money.

trinkets: small gifts.

venison: deer meat.

LISSA JOHNSTON was born in Alpine, Texas, and grew up in Dallas. She has a master's degree in history from The University of Texas at Arlington. She became interested in Cabeza de Vaca while reading a copy of his journal at the Special Collections Library at UTA. Ms. Johnston lives in Minnesota with her husband and two children.